PRAISE

for Cherie Kephart and
The Healing 100

"This multidimensional healing guide contains practical strategies and tools that anyone can use right away. It introduces a well-rounded collection of healing modalities all in one place in an easy to digest way. This book is a must-have resource for anyone looking to heal from within. As a health coach, this is an invaluable resource for me and my clients."

—Cindy Blaser, FDN-P
Holistic Health and Nutrition Coach

"Readers will find a rich treasure-trove of healing resources in this delightful, accessible work. Ms. Kephart writes with the voice of a compassionate survivor. Like a wise friend, she guides the reader through gentle healing practices that provide relief and hope."

—Gina Simmons Schneider, Ph.D., author of
*Frazzlebrain: Break Free from Anxiety, Anger and
Stress Using Advanced Discoveries in Neuropsychology*

"Within Cherie Kephart's comprehensive healing guide, I found resources that have, quite simply, improved my life!"
—Reina Menasche, *Licensed Clinical Social Worker* and author of *Silent Bird* and *Twice Begun*

"Cherie has compiled a comprehensive, fun list of healing modalities in accessible little wisdom nuggets. An inspiring collection of great reminders of how many different ways to help, heal, and live at our best."
—Debra Wanger, Certified Wellness Coach and author of *The Resilient Actor: How to Kick Ass in the Business Without it Kicking Your Ass*

"Healing is a multilevel process with many approaches and philosophies, but if you want to learn the best, learn from someone who's been there and done the work: Cherie Kephart, author of *A Few Minor Adjustments*."
—Matthew Pallamary, author of *Spirit Matters* and *The Center of The Universe Is Right Between Your Eyes But Home Is Where The Heart Is*

"What an excellent resource. It's unique, interesting, informative, and clear—all packaged with brilliant insight and a personal touch. I highly recommend this for everyone."
—Dr. Melinda Nevins, D.O.

"*The Healing 100* is an excellent resource of a well-researched collection of helpful modalities, practices, and tools. Cherie, through her amazing direct experiences from a myriad of health challenges, has thoughtfully compiled the many different ways you can help yourself heal."
—Willow MacPherson, Homeopathic Practitioner

THE HEALING 100

THE HEALING 100

A Practical Guide to Transforming Your Body, Mind, and Spirit

CHERIE KEPHART

BAZI
PUBLISHING

PUBLISHING

Bazi Publishing
San Diego, CA
BaziPublishing.com

For more information, email bazi@bazipublishing.com or visit BaziPublishing.com

PUBLISHER'S CATALOGING-IN-PUBLICATION DATA

Names: Kephart, Cherie, author.

Title: The healing 100 : a practical guide to transforming your body, mind, and spirit / Cherie Kephart.

Other titles: Kephart, Cherie. Few minor adjustments.

Description: San Diego, CA : Bazi Publishing, [2018] | Written as a companion guide to the author's "A few minor adjustments: a memoir of healing."

Identifiers: ISBN: 978-1-947127-06-7 (paperback) | 978-1-947127-07-4 (ePub) | 978-1-947127-08-1 (mobi) | LCCN: 2018943507

Subjects: LCSH: Mind and body. | Well-being. | Self-care, Health. | Healing--Psychological aspects. | Holistic medicine. | Holism. | Alternative medicine. | Chronic diseases--Diagnosis. | Chronic diseases--Alternative treatment. | Mind and body therapies. | Body-mind centering. | Spiritual life. | Change (Psychology) | Self-realization. | Self-actualization (Psychology) | BISAC: BODY, MIND & SPIRIT / Healing / General. | BODY, MIND & SPIRIT / Inspiration & Personal Growth. | BODY, MIND & SPIRIT / Reference. | HEALTH & FITNESS / Alternative Therapies. | HEALTH & FITNESS / Healing. | MEDICAL / Healing.

Classification: LCC: RA776.95 .K46 2018 | DDC: 615.5--dc23

Printed in the United States of America
10 9 8 7 6 5 4 3 2 1

Book Jacket & Interior Page Design: Asa Wild at asawild.org
Author's Photograph: Brigid Parsons

For all those who have helped me heal—
I am soaring because you cared.

Author's Notes

I wrote this book as a companion guide to my award-winning memoir, *A Few Minor Adjustments: A Memoir of Healing.* Since the release of my memoir, I have received an outpouring of heartfelt messages from readers inspired by my story. This powerful outreach has strengthened my passion to continue writing and sharing my experiences.

Who is this book for? It's for everyone in need of healing. Wait, isn't that everyone? Okay then, this book is for everyone.

And just like with my memoir, if you learn anything from this book and decide to abruptly change your life, it is not my fault. But any laughter you experience, I'll take credit for that.

Improving your health is
more than focusing just
on your health.
You improve it by focusing
on your whole life.

CONTENTS

Even the worst parts of
our lives can become
something meaningful.

Welcome to
The Healing 100

On tax day, April 15, 2004, when most of the United States was rushing to the post office before the tax deadline, I was being rushed to the hospital. At thirty-two years old, I collapsed in my shower, crawled to the phone, and called for help.

That was the start of my long, arduous journey with a chronic, mysterious illness.

Until that day, I was an athlete competing in beach volleyball, a runner racing in marathons to raise money for charities, a successful scientific and technical writer, and a world traveler who had been to more than forty countries. But all that came to an arresting halt.

I spent the next several years searching for answers. I had two goals: (1) find a diagnosis, and (2) try not to die. I had more than twenty symptoms, such as a rapid heart rate that raced up to 200 beats per minute while resting, neurological symptoms, intense neck pain, vertigo, debilitating fatigue, digestive issues, and more.

I went from doctor to doctor and underwent numerous tests, evaluations, and experimental treatments. I endured an exploratory heart procedure and tried medications, herbs, and supplements, taking up to forty-six pills a day. I even saw eccentric healers like a Russian ex-physicist who waved fertile chicken eggs over my chest to try and reset the erratic beat of my heart. I tried anything and everything people suggested I try.

After six years, I was bedridden, hallucinating, and being spoon fed. I was dying. The worst part was I didn't even know why. For the full harrowing and sometimes humorous story, check out my memoir, *A Few Minor Adjustments: A Memoir of Healing*.

Finally, I began to heal. Now, I am on the road to restored health. I'm often asked, "What helped you heal?" I always respond the same way: "It isn't just one thing, it's a hundred."

With that in mind, I'm excited to share with you what I call *The Healing 100*, the core one hundred healing modalities, remedies, and treatments that delivered me from the precipice of death, to truly living again. I have employed all of these healing techniques over many years, some for a short duration, and others that I still continue today. The one thing they all have in common is that they assisted me on my healing path.

Think of having a toolbox for your health. We all have one that we fill up with different tools throughout our lives, using each one as needed, depending on our circumstances. *The Healing 100* are my favorites—my essential tools. These are ones I know I wouldn't be alive, or sane, without.

Through my search for life-saving answers, I discovered that real healing is not just about healing the physical; it is about healing the body, mind, and spirit together. Without attention to fully restoring all three of these aspects of ourselves, we cannot completely heal. In addition, it is never about just one approach, one technique, or one remedy.

Healing at this deep level, becoming whole, vibrant, and free of *dis-ease*, calls for an assortment of tools. This guide focuses on all aspects of healing, highlighting several different techniques designed to bring about a return to total well-being.

Books could be, and have been, written about many of these one hundred tools. This guide serves as an invitation to try them, with the aspiration of creating a higher level of consciousness regarding health and the healing process.

Perhaps you will try only one tool, or you might try them all. Whatever you decide, I hope you'll keep an open mind and give them a chance. Everyone is different, so find what resonates with you and focus on those. Some of them may not be needed right now but may be useful later, or you may know someone who could benefit from them. It is also important to note that not every tool works for every person; if it doesn't feel like it is working for you, move on and try another one. Remember, different things work for different people.

Thank you for joining me on this journey. I am delighted to share with you all I have learned. Remember, healing starts with belief. Enjoy the process and believe that you can heal.

Wishing you the best of healing and happiness,

Cherie Kephart, author of
A Few Minor Adjustments: A Memoir of Healing

What is it to be healthy?
It's more than our physical
body. It's every thought.
Every action.
Every breath.
Healthy is all the decisions
we make, in every moment.

THE HEALING 100

LISTED ALPHABETICALLY

1 ⌒ ACUPUNCTURE AND ACUPRESSURE

Dating as far back as 100 BC, acupuncture is one of the oldest Chinese therapies designed to release pain and promote healing. It is rooted in the understanding that we are all made up of energy known as qi (or chi). Acupuncturists place slender needles into select parts of the body with the goal of clearing blockages and restoring balance to the flow of qi. Acupressure, another Chinese therapy designed to relieve pain and support healing, is achieved through physical pressure by a hand or device placed on particular points of the body. I have had excellent results from each; from calming my rapid heartbeat, to soothing muscle and joint pain, to boosting my immune system to help fight infection. Although I sometimes feel like a pin cushion, acupuncture is rarely painful, and mostly a relaxing, rejuvenating experience.

2 ⌒ AFFIRMATIONS

Just like your body has energy moving through and around it that affects your well-being, words also contain energy that can affect your experiences. Affirmations create a positive experience. Find affirmations that resonate with you. Even better, create your own. Be specific. Construct them in the present tense, as if they are already happening, and when you say your affirmations, be aware of how you feel. If you affirm, "I am strong," then focus on feeling strong. Here are some affirmations I have adopted that help me:

- I am happy, healthy, and full of energy

- I welcome kindness, laughter, and peace into my life

- I am healing and achieving optimal health

- I am loved and full of love

- The world is joyful and my life is a success

- I am safe

- I am at ease

- I am whole

- I am infinite

3 ◯ AIR PURIFIER

An air purifier is a machine that eliminates pollutants, toxins, and impurities from the air in a room or space. It can reduce or remove dust, dust-mite waste, mold spores, pet dander, smoke particles, and some bacteria and viruses. Air purifiers are especially beneficial for people with allergies and sensitivities. I sleep with one in my bedroom and run it on low all night. Ever since I started using it, my sinuses have cleared up; I sleep better, and I don't have a sore throat and dry eyes in the morning. Since there are many different kinds of air purifiers, do your research.

There are other ways to purify the air, like adding plants to your home or office. Not only will they increase the purity of the air, they are naturally calming and decorative. I love my plants, and I think they love me too. Himalayan pink salt lamps are also a wonderful addition to any space. They naturally purify the air by pulling toxins from the room and neutralizing them. I love my salt lamp just as much as I love my plants, and the bright orange glow is a beautiful bonus.

4 ⟳ ALLOPATHIC MEDICINE

As much as I prefer natural and organic ways of healing to allopathic (or Western) medicine, it is often a fundamental part of health. I believe that a combination of modalities promotes healing. The key is to figure out when you can use a more natural remedy or technique, and when you require a more mainstream, medicinal approach. As an example, I received a heart procedure that saved my life, and I am indeed grateful for all the staff, medicines, instruments, and techniques that went into that. Another time during my illness, I endured six months of IV antibiotics, steroids, and a host of other pharmaceuticals that also saved my life. Approaching your health with an open mind is imperative for any healing to occur. I wanted to cure myself naturally, and for a while, I was unwilling to use some forms of allopathic medicine. This reluctance almost killed me. I had to learn to be open to all possibilities. Whether choosing allopathic, natural, or a combination of the two, I am always sure to research, educate myself, and talk to professionals when exploring my options, so I can discern what is best for me.

5 ⊙ AROMATHERAPY AND ESSENTIAL OILS

Essential oils are highly concentrated, derived from plants, and useful to improve emotional, physical, and mental health. The practice of inhaling them, known as aromatherapy, can be emotionally and mentally therapeutic. When applied topically to the skin, they also have healing properties. I use lavender oil on my pillow and in my bath to help me relax and sleep, since lavender evokes calmness. When I have an upset stomach, bloating, or constipation, I rub a drop or two of pure peppermint oil on my stomach, which aids digestion. Using aromatherapy and essential oils is simple. Dilute a small amount in a base of water or oil, and apply it to your skin or inhale it. You can also diffuse, simmer, or use them in a lamp. Be sure to purchase pure oils that are 100% from botanical extracts, with no other ingredients, fragrances, or chemicals.

6 ⊙ ART THERAPY

Art therapy, also known as expressive art therapy, is the creation of meaningful and thought-provoking works of art without focusing on the result. The process of making art is the most important part. Engaging in art forms like ceramics, creative writing, drawing, jewelry making, needlepoint, painting, photography, or sculpting enables the imagination to flow freely. This de-emphasizes the attention on pain and illness, redirecting your energy toward a more relaxed and happier state. We are creative beings, so by expressing your creativity you are triggering positive brain function and a sense of well-being. For example, I love sea otters—I am not certain if they even know I exist, but my affinity for them remains unchanged—so I sketched one. I felt so happy doing it, and the sight of that sketch still makes me smile. Find what makes you happy, and start creating!

7 ⌒ BACH FLOWER ESSENCES

Bach flower essences were discovered by Dr. Edward Bach, a physician, pathologist, and bacteriologist. Each remedy is created from nature and designed to help overcome emotions like anxiety, depression, fear, guilt, resentment, shock, and others. I have found them to be safe, effective, and easy to use. First, identify the correct remedy by consulting with a flower essence practitioner or a health expert in your local health food store, or look online at Bachcentre.com.

Once you have identified the correct remedy, place a few drops of it under your tongue, and one drop on each wrist. Do this a couple of times a day until you notice a shift. These remedies also come with corresponding affirmations, which can increase their healing benefits. Over time, you may notice that you need certain remedies more often than others. I used to take *Pine* for guilt that I placed on myself for silly things. I was always too hard on myself, so I practically bathed in *Pine*. With the help of essences and the affirmations, I healed my tendency to beat myself up. I don't feel sucked into guilt anymore. I realized it is a useless emotion that doesn't help anyone. Find what you want to conquer most and try that. It is a beautiful experience to work through emotional and mental obstacles and leave them behind.

8 ⌒ BELIEVING

To heal, we need to *believe* that we can. Once you understand this, it's amazing what can happen. Since the body, mind, and emotions are intricately connected, you can't heal the body without shifting mentally and emotionally. I am proof that healing is possible. When I started living from a space of believing, I began to heal. I let go of the gloomy cloud looming over me. I decided the sun was going to shine on me, and once I believed that at my deepest core, it did. I encourage you to take this step, and believe, believe, believe.

9 ⌒ BEING ACCOUNTABLE

When I first became ill, I wanted to blame something for my illness: a pathogen, place, or person; anything other than myself. After years of introspection, I discovered there is no one and nothing to blame. It was a defining moment when I realized the part I played in my own *dis-ease*. No, I didn't go out looking for illness, nor did I wish for the pain and suffering that I went through. I especially didn't ask for the strange and dangerous health challenges I encountered living in Zambia as a Peace Corps volunteer. In retrospect, I realize it was my choice to take that position and move there.

I also contributed to my own ill health in a variety of other ways: living life too fast, exercising too much, not getting adequate nutrition, not getting enough sleep, suppressing my emotions, and a host of other bad habits. I learned that I had been too rigid and extreme. This is not to say that I needed to blame myself; quite the contrary. I simply needed to say to myself that I understand the things I have done and how they contributed to how sick and out of balance I became. I identified my role, my mistakes, and my missteps, and I thanked the person I used to be. Then I focused on how to make better choices to support myself as I moved on. I took accountability for my actions with compassion and love, enabling me to catapult forward.

10 ⌒ BEING OPEN

The willingness to try new things, listen to new ideas, and keep your heart open to the new possibilities is a valuable trait. If you close yourself off to life, your ability to heal will be considerably diminished. By being open, your life has a limitless number of possibilities. What better way to turn your life in a positive direction than to try something new? Since you are reading this book, my guess is that you are already willing to try new things. That's fantastic. Even the slightest opening to change and seeking new things can deliver a whole new realm of possibilities. It's always good to check in with your intuition before trying something new. A healer once had me wave fertile chicken eggs over my chest to reset the erratic beat of my heart. Did it work? Why did I do it? The full humbling and hilarious story is in my book, *A Few Minor Adjustments*. The point is, I learned so much and wouldn't change or take back that experience because I healed in other ways from it. You will be amazed at what can happen when you open yourself to new techniques, ideas, places, foods, and experiences. Who ever said healing can't be an adventure? Be inquisitive, challenge your thinking, and be open to the wondrous pageant that is life.

11 ⌒ BEING PRESENT

Being present is an important part of any healing process. We are almost always worried and not in the moment. When the mind is busy going over the past and planning for the future, it fatigues us. This creates stress. Balance is restored by engaging in activities that keep us in the moment. Being fully present is a key way to connect the body and mind. At first, this may seem challenging, but over time it becomes easier and offers great rewards. When I notice my mind wandering or worrying, I gently ease my thoughts back to the day before me. It gets easier the more you do it. Don't get down on yourself; like with most of these techniques, we are retraining our brains. Be gentle with yourself and know that whatever you are doing is good enough.

12 ⌒ BREATHING

Our breath is the bridge between our body and our mind. Every time we are tense, we hold our breath. Just breathing fully releases that tension. Learning to watch our breath teaches us to become more present and be able to slow down and control our mind from constantly over-thinking and worrying about something. Most of us are not breathing fully, deeply, and freely. I used to breathe shallow from my chest and was barely getting enough oxygen. I thought my body did everything for me and that I didn't need to do anything. Not true. Breathing is a voluntary as well as an involuntary process. To receive the full benefits from our breath, the first step is to practice being more aware of it. Try concentrating on it, even for just a minute a day. It is incredible what increasing the oxygen to your cells can do. There are breath therapists who can help. I have been to one who taught me better breathing techniques for both daily, mundane activities, as well as during meditation or stressful situations. Awareness is essential. Put a sign that says "Breathe" on your refrigerator, at your desk, or wherever you will see it. My doctor has one on her ceiling, so when her patients are lying down and receiving a treatment they see the sign and are reminded. Your breath is your life, so inhale and exhale with awareness and gratitude.

13 ⟲ BURNING RITUAL

A burning ritual is an ancient method of releasing what no longer serves us. Gather up any documents, letters, old medical information, and anything else that has negative energy that you want to let go of. Don't burn anything you may need, like your driver's license just because the DMV snapped an unflattering photo of you. This is solely for items no longer needed that can disappear without consequences. Trust your instincts. If you don't have anything physical, make a list of everything you want to let go of that is causing you harm, and burn that list. I once burned more than 250 pages of EKG readings after my heart procedure. Another time I burned my old medical records from my time in Africa with a note of gratitude for all I had learned.

If possible, use an outdoor fireplace or a bonfire pit and piece by piece witness your past go up in flames to be carried away by the wind. Be sure to light the fire with full awareness. At the end, express gratitude for all the cleansing and abundance you have in your life.

14 ⟲ BURNING SAGE

Practiced by many cultures all over the world, the ritual of burning sage is a sacred, spiritual way to cleanse and purify a person, a group, or a space, and it can provide improved clarity and wisdom. Think of the word "sage," or "sagely," and what it means: perceptive, wise, and sagacious. Burning sage can help clear the energy in your home or office, or around your body. I do it whenever I feel like I need cleansing from any aspect of my life. It's easy to do: Take a dried sage bundle and place it on a heat-safe surface and light the front tip of it until it smokes. If it flames, gently blow on it until only embers and smoke are present. Use your hand to wave the smoke around your body and to all corners of your house—unless you have super-sensitive smoke alarms. While doing this, focus on the negative aspects leaving your life. Feel them being replaced with positive, healing energy.

15 ⌒ CARINGBRIDGE

A non-profit organization, CaringBridge is dedicated to helping those enduring physical, mental, and emotional trials by providing an online resource to receive encouragement, hope, and love. I turned to CaringBridge when I was bedridden and struggling to stay alive. It was an invaluable tool that boosted my spirits and helped me feel cared for. I used it to reach out to my friends and family and keep them updated on what was happening to me. When I was too sick to manage it, my boyfriend and friends did, so everyone could be updated on my condition and check in with me, which not only helped me, but also helped my boyfriend, since everyone who called, emailed, etc. wanted to know my status. Instead of relaying the same information to different people several times a day, it was posted on CaringBridge so everyone could stay up to date. Check it out at Caringbridge.org.

16 ⌒ CHI MACHINE

A Chi Machine massages and stimulates the nervous system and helps provide an increased flow of oxygen to the lungs. It is said to improve blood flow, expand the functioning of the immune system and internal organs, and stimulate the lymphatic system, which is imperative for detoxification. It's simple to use. You lie down with your feet in the cradle of the device and switch it on. The machine slides from side to side, moving you with it. I did this for years when I had trouble walking and it was quite beneficial, since at the time I wasn't getting any exercise and my body felt stiff and stagnant. The sensation is much like being rocked back and forth in a chair or a swing, but with tighter, smaller movements. You can research and purchase Chi Machines online. Rebounders (mini trampolines) are also effective for activating the lymphatic system and increasing the flow of energy through the body. Put on some leg warmers, blast tunes from the 1980s, and have some fun.

17 ⭘ CHIROPRACTIC AND CRANIAL SACRAL THERAPY

Both chiropractic and cranial sacral therapies focus on adjusting the musculo-skeletal structure and nervous system to help restore and maintain health. The nervous system is the center of communication for your body and needs to be in balance for optimal wellness. Chiropractors use hands-on spinal manipulation to realign your body so it can do its job properly. Cranial sacral therapy is more subtle than a typical chiropractic adjustment. It is guided by movements that release compression in the head, sacrum, and spine, reducing stress and pain. Since 1992, I've endured chronic neck pain from a car accident, and although I sometimes feel like a pretzel when I'm being adjusted, both therapies have reduced my pain and realigned my body so I can better enjoy life.

18 ⭘ COMPASSION

Compassion is a beautiful gift. By feeling compassion for those who are suffering, we open up a pathway of connection filled with light and love. By expressing heartfelt kindness and concern, we unlock a door to healing in all aspects of our being. One aspect of cultivating compassion that is often overlooked is self-compassion. Having compassion for ourselves is vital for our well-being, something that took me years to practice. I have learned to give myself as much loving-kindness as I would for my grandmother, cat, or best friend. I then feel lighter, more peaceful, and grateful to embody such renewed self-love.

19 ⌒ COUNSELING

At some point along my healing path I discovered that talking with my friends and family was useful, necessary, and loving, but not enough. My traumas were too great and my illness too severe. I needed to purge my destructive self-talk, my pent-up emotions, and the crazy narrative swarming in my head. I wanted to find someone who would listen without judgment, and who was dedicated to helping me sift through my wounds and triumph over them. When I reached out and found a counselor I connected with, it was a revelation. Looking back on all that time spent opening up and acknowledging my pain, I realize it helped me release it, restore my love for myself, and find the courage to leave my pain behind and move onward.

20 ⌒ CRYING

Crying can be a powerful way to discharge built-up emotions. If you ever feel the urge to cry, give in to the body's need for release. Don't judge or stop it. Just let it out (unless you are in the middle of an important interview or on a first date). If you have trouble getting the tears to flow, play some melancholy mood music like "Crying" by Roy Orbison, "I'm So Lonesome I Could Cry" by Hank Williams, or "Everybody Hurts" by R.E.M. You can also watch a tearjerker movie. Some of my favorites are *Dead Poets Society, E.T., I Am Sam, Good Will Hunting, Rain Man, Rudy, Shawshank Redemption,* or *Up.* However you get there, be grateful for and appreciate the release. It is indeed healing.

21 ○ DANCING

Whenever I feel up to it, I turn on my favorite music and dance. If you are physically limited, you can dictate how much or little you do. If I only feel like doing one song, that is all I do. Even if you don't have the energy to stand, try dancing in your chair or from the couch. Tap your feet, sway from side to side, and move your arms. Moving your physical body can also move your emotional body and release suppressed emotions that contribute to your symptoms.

The benefit is akin to other forms of exercise, and you just may smile while you are at it. Some songs that always get me up out of my chair are "December 1963 (Oh What a Night)" by The Four Seasons, "Footloose" by Kenny Loggins, "Happy" by Pharrell Williams, "Kiss" by Prince and The Revolution, "You Make My Dreams" by Daryl Hall and John Oates, and my absolute favorite song of all time to dance to, "Build Me Up Buttercup" by The Foundations. I also like to explore new music and explore different moves. Although I haven't mastered breakdancing or the moonwalk, nor can I dance en pointe, I *can* pretend I'm a ballerina or a modern dance professional, gliding from room to room wearing a big smile.

22 ○ DOUBLING DOWN

"Double down" is a card-playing term that I give a different meaning to. In blackjack, to double down means to double your bet and receive an additional card. In my spin on the term, it means that whenever you have an adverse circumstance that brings you unhappiness, find two things that are positive about it to counter the negativity. My close friend Christine died from breast cancer at age forty-three. While weak and shaking, I told my doctor about losing my friend. She listened intently then responded, "I know it's very tough and there is much sorrow and pain. The trick is to find the beauty." At first I was mad at this suggestion. I then realized there is beauty in everything, so I thought about two positives. First, although Christine died, I was able to remember how well she lived and the lives she inspired. Second, I got to witness how her amazing husband was always there for her. I am now dear friends with him, and we help support each other. He understands illness and is always there for me too. Christine's death brought us together as close friends, and for that I am grateful. The more complex and painful the negative, the more powerful the two positives need to be. This technique always helps me combat the most trying of circumstances.

23 ○ ELIMINATING CLUTTER

By eliminating clutter and simplifying your home, you can clear your mind and relax your spirit. Donating, recycling, and letting go of what you no longer use or need is a positive way to help others and promote a healthier living environment that can help you relax and improve your energy. Everything in your environment is best if it is positive, neutral, and/or functional. If there is anything that has an undesirable memory or energy attached to it, let it go. I had a skirt that I wore while delivering the eulogy at a friend's funeral. It fit me perfectly, but I no longer wanted to wear it because it reminded me of his death, not his life, so I donated it. Someone else would enjoy it and bring a more positive energy to it. You may feel lighter and more present by letting go of what no longer serves you. Your house is meant to be a peaceful, positive place, and ever-changing with your life. Keep it current, clean, free of clutter, and full of happy memories and energy. By doing this, you can help shift your energy into something more uplifting and positive. Conquering clutter on the outside helps you conquer emotional disharmony and clutter on the inside.

24 ᴼ ELIMINATING CERTAIN FOODS

Foods can heal us, but for some people, consuming certain types of foods contribute to ill health. Some of the most common foods that cause allergies, sensitivities, or disease are corn, dairy, gluten, soy, and sugar. By cutting out harmful foods, you can heal in dramatic ways. To discern which foods are detrimental to your health, eliminate one food at a time. After a few weeks, add it back and notice if you feel differently. Keeping a daily journal of what you eat and how you react to each meal/food will help you determine which foods are lowering your energy or causing you pain. It's a slow process, but it is extremely liberating and rewarding when you are finally able to deduce what causes you pain and fatigue.

25 ⌀ ENERGETIC KINESIOLOGY

Energetic kinesiology is a hands-on holistic approach to healing that aims to identify imbalance, pain, and stress in the body and to restore homeostasis. Through strength techniques known as muscle testing, a practitioner of kinesiology works to establish brain integration and emotional equilibrium. It is an emerging field in alternative medicine and complements a host of other modalities. I recently started seeing a kinesiologist who works at my rheumatologist's office. After only a few short hours, I noticed a shift in my energy, and my brain felt more balanced and alert.

26 ⌀ EPSOM SALT AND SEA SALT BATHS

A warm bath with Epsom salt can reduce inflammation and alleviate muscle pain and tension because of its rich magnesium content. Salt water discharges negative ions, which is why diving in the ocean can feel so uplifting. The combination of Epsom salt and sea salt also has detoxification benefits. Since I have a heart condition, I am careful not to heat the water too hot or stay in too long. About ten to fifteen minutes once or twice a week is enough for me.

27 ⌀ FENG SHUI

Feng shui is a Chinese system of principles that govern the orientation and design of belongings, homes, and buildings. It is based upon the belief that design and orientation directly affect the flow of energy known as qi (or chi). The aim is to harmonize the environment, resulting in a more balanced life. It can be fun to experiment with this and see how it feels. I once hired a friend skilled in feng shui to help balance my home. We decluttered bookshelves and closets, added plants, rock gardens, mirrors, candles, and rearranged furniture. I replaced my cheap rubber doorstops with beautiful blue hunks of crystal. It didn't cost much, and I loved the results. The space flowed better, and I felt happier and more at peace.

28 ⌒ FLIPPING A COIN

Having health challenges can compromise our ability to make decisions. Have a tough decision to make? Try flipping a coin. I know—*what? Am I crazy?* No. Actually, this is an ingenious twist on the standard coin flip; a technique to help people like me who are in our minds way too much. I often have trouble making decisions, especially big ones, and I often have lots of decisions related to my health. Do I try a new remedy, a new treatment, or a move to Greenland?

First, think of a decision you are faced with, grab a coin, and place it in your hand. Assign *Heads* to one decision and *Tails* to the other. For example, if you are pondering moving to Greenland, pick *Heads* for "Yes, I am definitely moving to Greenland," and *Tails* for "No." Now that you've assigned the coin, close your eyes and think about your choice and the sides you assigned, and pay close attention to what happens next.

Once you feel ready, open your eyes and flip the coin, catching it with your hand and closing your other hand around it without looking at it. Instead of looking at the coin to determine what you should do, think about the moments before and during the flip, and how you felt while anxiously waiting to see if you need to go to REI to by a wool parka for your relocation to the icy North. What side did you hope it would land on?

You don't need to see how the coin actually landed. You already know the answer to your decision by what you hoped would happen. Next time you are faced with a tough decision, try it. It may just show you what you really want and/or what your body needs.

29 ○ FOCUSING ON WHAT YOU CAN DO

Focus on what you can do, not on what you can't. If you focus your attention on what you are unable to do, or you spend your energy feeling sad and angry and complaining about what you used to be able to do, you will remain in a depressed and damaging state, always longing for what you don't have. There is a healthy period of grieving that's necessary when we lose a part of our lives or our abilities. Once that is done, we need to move forward. By focusing your attention on the talents, skills, and physical and mental abilities you *do* have, you will feel confident and upbeat, and you will ultimately increase your mental and emotional well-being. When I think about how I can't run or play beach volleyball anymore, I remember that I can still run errands, and I can still go to the beach and nestle my feet in the sand. We all have limitations. The trick is to look outside those and enjoy what we are still able to do. It may not be exactly what we want, but with the right focus and appreciation, it can be fulfilling.

30 ○ FOOT PATCHES

Detoxification is an important part of our body's natural process. The lymphatic system, which consists of lymph nodes, the spleen, thymus, and tonsils, is designed to remove waste and toxins from the body. Sometimes our lymphatic system needs help, especially when we are ill, or over-exposed to toxins. Foot patches remove toxins and assist the lymphatic system. When I first heard of friends using foot patches, I didn't believe they worked. Then I became toxic after a negative reaction to an antibiotic. I had numerous neurological symptoms, including neuropathy in both arms and legs, which went on for months. My doctor said I was toxic from the medication and needed to detox, but nothing I tried helped until I used special gold foot patches from Japan. Within two weeks, my symptoms dramatically decreased, and at the end of two months, almost all my symptoms were gone. The best way to use them is while you sleep, wearing socks over them. In the morning, remove and discard the used patches and wash your feet. Not all foot patches are created equal; do your research and find ones that work for you. You will never know whether something works until you try it.

31 ⟲ FORGIVENESS

Forgiving others is a critical part of healing old wounds. By holding on to anger, resentment, or blame, we harm ourselves by harboring a negative, debilitating buildup of emotions. When we learn to forgive, we find a lighter, healthier path for ourselves and those we love. The most difficult person to forgive is often you. I endured a horrific incident in my early twenties, and for years I not only blamed the perpetrators, I blamed myself. It took lots of introspection to forgive the perpetrators, and it took even more to forgive myself. By remembering that we are all human and we all misstep, and by forgiving ourselves and others, we can release that toxic energy and gift ourselves the freedom to move forward, make amends, and ultimately make healthier choices. Remember, to forgive means to love.

32 ◯ Friends

Your friends are your best resource. Don't be afraid to ask for help, love, and support. You'd do it for them. Think Beatles: "With a Little Help From My Friends." Don't like the Beatles? Wait, who doesn't like the Beatles? What about "Lean on Me" by Bill Withers? People need people, so reach out to those who care for you, or make new friends who better understand your plight. I've met some of my dearest friends while in the IV room, each of us of hooked up to a stream of medication. This support may help you navigate uncharted territory. They just may have the advice, wisdom, and kind words you need, and you can share your unique set of knowledge and encouragement to help them.

33 ◯ Fun

For many years, I spent all my time searching for a diagnosis and cure to my unknown illness. After years of suffering, a theme emerged from all my practitioners, my counselor, and my friends. They all started to ask, "What do you do for fun?" I scoffed. "Fun? I'm trying not to die. Who can think about fun?" It took a while before I understood that having fun could help me heal. More interestingly, I had literally forgotten how to have fun. I embarked on a quest of spending quality time each day doing something that made me happy, something I did for the pure joy of it, not related to my illness, to-do lists, or goals. I had to relearn what made me happy. With my new circumstances, it was harder than I thought, but now, I practice fun every day. I wouldn't be this happy or healthy without it. What is fun to me now? Abstract painting, creative writing, working on jigsaw puzzles, playing goofy board games with friends, discovering a new healthy restaurant, watching uplifting movies, creating new tasty recipes, and most of all, taking time out of my day to simply be silly and find new things that bring me joy.

34 ⟳ GOING WITH THE FLOW

Are you resisting what is presented to you and forcing your way through life? Are you trying to control your environment and the outcomes of every detail of your life? If so, you will run into obstacles, resistance, and pain. I still struggle with this from time to time, but now I practice relaxing into the natural flow of life more than ever. Going with the flow isn't just an expression. There are patterns to flowing energy, and when we align ourselves with it, everything feels easier. It's almost as if we are being assisted.

When I am in the flow of life, I am more at ease; opportunities open, and I feel more connected to everything and everyone. Pause and ask yourself, "Am I going with the flow, or am I trying to control my situation?" When you go with the flow, you may arrive at your destination with more ease, more grace, and a more balanced body, mind, and spirit.

35 ⟳ GRATITUDE

Gratitude is a powerful healing tool. I cannot emphasize enough how important gratitude is for creating a healthy and vibrant life. I'm not simply talking about thanking someone for passing you the salt, although being grateful for small things is important too. What I'm talking about is practicing sincere and deep gratitude. Science has shown the many benefits of gratitude on the brain and overall health.

By learning to cultivate genuine gratitude for both the beautiful and the dark parts of your life, you can see the lessons behind the unsavory aspects of being human. You can then grow and move forward with a renewed belief that all of it happened to help and support you. If you take away only one tool from *The Healing 100*, let it be this one. With that in mind, thank you for reading this book and allowing me to share my experiences with you.

36 ⟳ GRIEVING

Losing your health is a loss as significant as losing someone you love. Grief is a powerful emotion associated with losing love, a loved one, or a loved aspect of our life. Embracing grief is a crucial part of healing from loss. By allowing yourself to grieve and fully acknowledge your feelings, you can heal from a deep place. When I finally let myself grieve all I had lost because of my illness, I gained compassion for myself and felt stronger and more at peace. It was a process that took time, but it was beautiful how open my heart became as I did it. Be kind to yourself, and allow yourself the space and time to grieve.

37 ⟳ GROUNDING

The simple act of walking barefoot in the dirt, grass, or sand brings our bodies back to our most natural state. We are not meant to walk with shoes and socks, or with carpet, concrete, plastic, or metal beneath us. The earth provides electrons that increase the functioning of the immune and nervous systems, and that improve circulation. I always feel calmer and more grounded when I'm in contact with the earth. I do wear shoes to most places, but whenever I get the chance, I take off my shoes. The TSA knows what I'm talking about.

38 ⌒ HIGHER WAYS

There's a quote attributed to Albert Einstein that says, "Problems cannot be solved at the same level of awareness that created them." When you have a problem, look for higher ways to fix it. Change your frequency and change the way you are looking to resolve the problem. When you go to a higher level of consciousness about what is happening in your life, you will have a wider, clearer perspective and be able to see a solution. I've employed this perspective countless times. One example is when I was trying to figure out why my stomach was frequently bloated. I kept looking at the food I was eating. Which would make sense. I was angry that I couldn't figure out the cause. But it wasn't food. I finally let go of my ideas of what would cause bloating and most importantly, I also let go of my anger. I shifted to a higher frequency and took a step back. From a neutral space, I explored other habits I had. It turns out it was gum. I was chewing healthy, xylitol gum, thinking it was good for my teeth, but it was generating gas. I stopped chewing gum and my bloating significantly reduced. By looking at your life from a different vantage point, you can discover much more.

39 ⌒ HOMEOPATHY

Homeopathy is a holistic method of healing that uses naturally-occurring ingredients to help the body, mind, and spirit regain balance. It is based on the understanding that "like cures like." Before the onset of my sickness, I completed a two-year course on it and have used its remedies throughout my illness for physical, emotional, mental, and spiritual well-being. Homeopaths have a wealth of knowledge to help you identify the many layers of your illness and the remedies to meet your specific needs. There are hundreds of remedies for all types of ailments, physical, mental, and emotional. For example, I use arnica, a plant in the sunflower family, to soothe muscle pain and reduce inflammation, and I use ignatia, which is derived from the seeds of a bean tree, for overcoming grief and anxiety. The remedies are easy to use. Once you've identified the correct remedy by consulting with a homeopath, health expert in your local health food store, or naturopathic practitioner, you place three to five pellets underneath your tongue. The pellets dissolve and trigger the body's response to heal.

40 ○ HYPNOTHERAPY

Hypnotherapy is a technique that is often used to alter mental and emotional behaviors, attitudes, and several conditions like stress, anxiety, and pain. I'm not talking about hypnosis shows, although they can be quite entertaining; I once saw a guy take an enormous bite out of an onion without flinching, believing it was an orange. Hypnotherapy is a type of psychotherapy that reaches the subconscious to elevate emotions, thoughts, and behaviors to more conscious levels. I found it to be a powerful methodology for reaching new degrees of relaxation during some of the most stressful and painful times of my illness.

41 ◯ HUA

HUA (or Hooah) has several meanings. Many say it was originally military slang that meant "Heard, Understood, and Acknowledged." A more creative, urban use of this term is "Head Up Ass," referring to someone who is oblivious to their surroundings and the ramifications of their actions. Although I'm partial to the last one, I prefer to use a derivation of the military meaning: Heard, Understood, and Appreciated. All of us want HUA in our lives. When you speak your truth, you feel vindicated and confident that your life matters. When others understand what you are going through, you no longer feel alone. You feel supported, comforted, and loved. When you are appreciated, you feel that your efforts, however big or small, are valued. Feeling heard, understood, and appreciated improves self-esteem and gives us the boost we need to heal. With more energy, we can heal. What's the best way to get more HUA in your life? Give some. The more we give, the more we receive. Have fun with it. You may be surprised at what can happen when you have HUA in your life.

42 ◯ HULA-HOOPING

Laugh if you must (which I am okay with, since laughter is healing), but I bought a Hula-Hoop after trying it with my nephew. This type of movement is a good workout for the core muscles of my body that became stagnant throughout my illness. I put on some music, burn some calories, strengthen my heart, and have fun. Sure, I can only last a few minutes, but I am building up my stamina, and although I may look silly, I feel happy doing it. While you're at it, try jumping rope, table tennis, or tossing a Frisbee. If you want the Frisbee to come back, get a partner, or try a boomerang.

43 ○ INFRARED LIGHT

When infrared light is used as a tool for health, it is often in the form of far infrared rays (FIR). These rays cannot be seen by the naked eye, but they go deep into the body, expanding the cells and stimulating blood flow. Using them increases the regeneration of body tissue, repairing the nervous system. This destroys harmful free radicals and aids in the elimination of bodily waste. Some doctors offer infrared saunas as part of their therapeutic treatments. You can also purchase an infrared sauna, or an infrared dome, which is much smaller than a sauna and much less expensive. I use it over whatever part of my body needs healing, including my knees, stomach, back, and chest. I often read, watch a movie, meditate, or nap while using it since it's so relaxing. The dome fits comfortably over my lap, or my body while lying on the floor or in bed. I bought mine from my doctor who uses a lot of cutting-edge technology. They can also be found online. My dome has helped me reduce inflammation while shrinking fibroids and cysts. As with anything, research, start slow, and follow safety precautions like protecting your eyes.

44 ○ IRON INFUSIONS

Intravenous (IV) iron infusions are a way of transporting iron to a patient. This is a specific medical practice for people who are very low in iron. A simple blood test will measure how much iron is in your blood. My level was dangerously low and I had to receive these infusions, which helped tremendously. *Iron*ically (ha, get it?), while I was receiving IVs to replenish my low iron, I often sat next to a man who was getting IVs to remove the excess iron he had. Men typically have higher iron levels, and women tend to have lower, since we generally don't eat as much meat, and because we menstruate. Now I can maintain my iron levels without the IVs, so I would only recommend infusions if you absolutely need them. There are liquid iron supplements and other ways to boost your iron, but increasing your iron levels can be tricky because some people have an inability to absorb the iron or have digestion barricades. In all cases, it's best to get tested and consult with a doctor to find the right path for you.

45 ⟳ IV THERAPY

Intravenous (IV) therapy is a way to transport vitamins, minerals, and medications to a patient. The idea behind IV therapy can be either to boost your immune system and restore vitamin and mineral deficiencies, or to bypass the digestive system to administer needed pharmaceuticals. For six months, I did IV therapy to eliminate a chronic bacterial infection. I also received IV therapies for vitamins and minerals, something my body required for more than a few years because I was so depleted of nutrients. For this treatment, I went to a doctor who specialized in herbs and microbiology, and then to a rheumatologist.

46 ⟳ JOURNALING

Journaling can be a way of thinking things through. It helps purge pent-up emotions and harmful self-talk that we need to let go of. Although journaling is wonderful for helping us clear our minds of negativity, it is also useful when you are feeling well. Describe what you are grateful for and how you want your life to be going forward. Focus on the positives like continued healing and more peace of mind. Whatever you want to feel or be, write it down. Putting these thoughts on paper will solidify your needs and dreams. If you don't like writing, try an art journal, coloring in your words, or using cutouts from magazines. Be creative and have fun.

If you struggle with writing down your thoughts, try one of my simple twists that helped me let go of self-judgment. Grab a journal or stack of blank paper and a pen that is out of ink and use it to journal with. By doing that, you are practicing the same exercise as journaling, but there are no words to read and nothing evidential to berate yourself with. It also saves paper, since you can write over and over again on the same page. Think of the positive environmental impact! If you like to journal by typing, change your font color to white. You will still be typing, but you won't see the words. When you are finished, delete the file. You can also journal with your less dominant hand, which uses the opposite side of your brain and helps you tap into different emotions and thoughts. If you have to see words and use your dominant hand, try journaling with a fun color of ink like purple, or use a decorative pen and beautiful paper.

47 ◯ JUICING AND SMOOTHIES

Juicing, extracting the juice from fruits and vegetables, usually by putting them though a blender cycle, is an excellent way to add the nutritional benefits of fruits and vegetables. Use organic produce and a variety of vegetables and fruits so you can get a host of different vitamins and nutrients. Leaving the skins on certain fruits and vegetables, such as apples, carrots, and citrus fruits, can add more fiber and nutrients. When I started drinking homemade fruit smoothies and green juices, I noticed an instant boost in my energy and assistance with my digestion. I also contracted fewer colds and flus. It's also a great way to get nourishment when you don't feel like eating. I've always loved fruits and vegetables, but I didn't start drinking them until my thirties. My body now craves them, and I can't imagine my life without them.

48 ⌒ KNOWING YOUR ABCS

This is a brilliant technique I learned from my shamanic healer. In any given moment, you need to know your ABCs. A = Aware. B = Be. C = Choose. So, Aware, Be, and Choose in each moment, particularly when you are struggling. Take the first step, A, and raise your awareness to whatever situation you are faced with. When you become aware, take the second step, B, and just be. Don't try to change, cajole, or control anything, simply be with the circumstance and whatever emotions you experience. Once you feel calm, clear-minded, and ready, take the third step, C, and choose the next action that feels positive and healing. By remembering your ABCs, you can turn unsettling moments into transformative ones.

49 ⌒ LAUGHING

Throughout the duration of my illness, especially in the beginning, I had trouble laughing, so I started watching more comedies and tried to focus on funny and uplifting matters. My grandmother always said, "There is nothing so terrible that we can't laugh." Taking her sage advice, I try not to take myself too seriously. I actually create happy situations and enjoy being silly.

There is a direct correlation between our ability to laugh and our ability to embrace our feelings of sadness and be okay with them. A sense of humor is a profound way of coping with challenges. For instance, I'm laughing as I write this, picturing all of you readers wearing Underoos (if you don't know what they are, you may be entertained if you do a little research). To be fair, you can imagine me, the author, wearing a Wonder Woman outfit. Or switch it around. I'll wear the Underoos (and I've never owned a pair, or want to) and you the Wonder Woman or Superman outfit. The point is, laughter is a truly powerful medicine.

50 ◯ LAUGHTER YOGA

Different than laughing because something strikes you as humorous, Laughter Yoga is literally about laughing for no reason. This practice is about setting aside a specified time to laugh voluntarily, supporting the idea that laughter affects every aspect of our being. Laughter Yoga is usually done in groups, but I also do it at home, by myself, with a friend, or even over the phone. I simply set a timer and start laughing until the timer sounds. It is a little odd at first, but once you start laughing, and someone else laughs, you are soon laughing hard, and it feels good. Often when I'm with people, I do it longer than the timer. It's easiest to start with just one minute and with someone you know and feel comfortable with, not the checkout guy at the grocery store or your accountant. That's a little more advanced.

51 ◯ LETTING GO

Healing on an emotional level always encompasses letting go. As hard as it can be to let go of something, it is an expansive process. Whether it is an old article of clothing, a belief, a habit, or a damaging relationship, letting go not only releases you from the past, but it clears space, enabling you to experience the present more fully. When my health plummeted, I had to let go of labels that I thought were my identity: runner, beach volleyball player, world traveler, vegetarian. Because of my health challenges, I couldn't be these things anymore. When I let go of the need to be anything, I felt free. I had to learn to adapt and not get attached to any part of my life, because change is required for healing. Start first by letting go of small things, then grow your practice to include releasing all that does not serve you, bring joy to you, or make you feel whole. This cultivates new freedom and space in your life. Just when you think you've let everything go that you need to, you'll discover there is always more to let go of.

52 ◯ LISTENING TO YOUR BODY

It is said that open and loving communication is crucial for healthy relationships. One relationship that can benefit the most from this is the relationship we have with our body. Think about it. Our body conducts millions of processes each day without us even knowing what they are and how they work. I realize that some of you were napping in biology class, but it was one of my favorite subjects. Trust me, the body knows what it needs. Symptoms are signals that let us know that our body is out of balance. It is as if our body is screaming, "Pay attention!" When we ignore the little symptoms, they become major imbalances. When we have pain, it is the body saying, "Hey, what you are doing is hurting me." We often mask and suppress our symptoms with Band-Aids of all sorts, and we continue doing whatever hurts us. For example, temporary pain relief, including over-the-counter drugs, alcohol, tobacco, and even food can harm us and keep us from true healing. I was an expert at suppressing my pain. I didn't use alcohol or drugs, but I used food, exercise, and work, and I became an expert at ignoring my symptoms. Mind over matter, I thought. I forced myself, pushed hard, disregarded the pain and symptoms, and continued with all my bad habits. Ultimately, I paid for it. Now, I listen! I love my body and give it what it asks for.

53 ⁓ Love with Lipstick

When I was bedridden and wasting away with *goodness knows what* illness, my outlook became grim. I was sinking into a darkness that I didn't think I could return from. I was on my way out—then I had an idea. I asked a friend to buy me some cheap lipstick in a variety of colors. When she returned, she helped me limp over to my large bedroom and bathroom mirrors. Propped up against the counter, I took one of the lipsticks, and in bright burgundy I wrote, "You can do this." It didn't take long for my friend to grab a deep shade of red and write, "Believe."

By the end of the weekend, I had messages all over my mirrors in lipstick from my friends and family. The tremendous amount of time I spent in bed staring at the ceiling and walls was now replaced by reading the loving and encouraging messages all over the mirrors. Any time I went to the mirror, I no longer saw my withered face staring back. I saw love.

Be creative; use lipstick, or soap, or some other way to decorate your surroundings so that people can sign and write special messages to you. When you are feeling lonely, scared, or unsure, you can read them and feel supported and loved.

54 ⟳ MASSAGE

When my body aches, massage is one of the most therapeutic techniques I have ever experienced. Whether I get a professional massage, or I simply massage my aching forearms, neck, or feet, the release of stress and increased circulation always makes me feel better. There are several types of massage. Swedish, therapeutic, and lymphatic massages are the most gentle and healing for those with physical pain and illness. It can be fun too, trading massages with your significant other. Everyone is happy. Special note: If you are just coming down with a virus, influenza, or possible bacterial infection, it may not be the best time to get a massage. On rare occasions, a massage can drive it deeper.

55 ⟳ MEDITATION

Meditation is a powerful healing practice. For me, it has been the cornerstone to healing my full being. There is a broad spectrum of ways to meditate, including meditating while sitting in silence, or while eating, walking, or listening to guided meditations. Different meditations are geared toward different spiritual practices. It's much more than just sitting still and contemplating your belly button. You don't have to live in an ashram in the Himalayas to meditate, nor do you have to use advanced techniques. It was during meditation that I discovered a part of myself that was able to watch the drama I was in and to arrive at peace.

Here are some simple suggestions: Create a quiet, natural space where you feel comfortable and free of distractions.

Concentration is the first step of meditation. The breath is a wonderful focus because it is the bridge that connects the body to the mind. Meditating may be difficult in the beginning. When trying to stay focused on our breath, we usually find the mind wanders. This is normal. With practice, the mind quiets down. As we learn to concentrate and become more present, we start to discover hidden realms of ourselves.

Some aids that may be helpful are meditation CDs, an online series, apps like *Insight Timer*, or getting out and joining a class and meeting like-minded people. Once you try it, you may be hooked, just like me!

56 ○ Movement

Movement is therapeutic. My wise and caring osteopath always says, "Move your body every day in every way," and that "motion is lotion." Let yourself feel free and move your body in all directions with ease and grace. Do what feels natural and comfortable without overextending or overdoing. Little movements every day can make a big difference. Consider gentle exercises like qi gong and tai chi, both thought of as meditating while moving. Both are gentle and can assist in alleviating ill health. Whatever you try, go slow and find what feels right for you.

57 ○ Muscle Activation Therapy (MAT)

Muscle activation therapy (also known as muscle activation technique) is not the same as physical therapy or chiropractic work. A MAT therapist will specifically identify and correct imbalances of muscles and instability of joints related to injury or illness. The emphasis is on finding the areas of weakness and identifying positions that increase joint motion and improve stability. The MAT therapist I worked with helped me restore strength in my legs, shoulders, and neck that had atrophied from my condition.

58 ◯ MUSIC

Two things that all cultures have in common are language and music. Music is an integrated part of our humanness and joy, and it is important for healing. Different types of music can help with emotions or situations that challenge you. Sometimes classical or spa-type music can soothe. Sometimes you need a boost instead.

When I was feeling exceptionally sad because of my bleak circumstances, I decided to change my mood by creating a playlist called *Happy Tunes*. I compiled fifteen of the most upbeat, happy songs I could find. When I heard them, I could not help but feel happy! Not only did the research for this little project bring me lots of happiness, but the result was uplifting. Sharing *Happy Tunes* with my friends uplifted them as well. Create your own playlist, keep it handy, and share it with your friends. Depending on your taste in music, they may just thank you.

59 ◯ NATURE

I love to get up close and personal with nature. Whether going to the beach, going for a walk, sitting in a park, or smelling the flowers in your backyard, it will promote relaxation and well-being. But I don't stop there. I bring nature into my house with plants, flowers, and stones. Right now I have day lilies waving at me and the aroma of freshly picked peach roses caressing my senses. Keeping connected to nature is a wonderful way to bring your body back to its natural state of being. Explore and have fun!

60 ⌒ NEUROFEEDBACK

Neurofeedback, also called EEG biofeedback, is the electronic retraining of brain activity. It's like physical therapy for the brain. My rheumatologist offered it in his clinic. Sessions lasted about one hour, twice a week, for six months. On the initial visit, electrodes were affixed all over my head and hooked up to a monitoring machine. Then, readings were taken of my brain activity. With this baseline, the technician programmed the machine to retrain the areas in my brain that were suffering, out of sync, damaged, or not performing well. The changes in me were dramatic.

When I started neurofeedback, my physical body was beginning to heal, but I still suffered from extreme anxiety and fear, sadness, nervousness, neurological sensitivities, and PTSD from past trauma. By the end of the six months, I felt calmer and more interested in being out in the world again. I had less mental chatter and negative thoughts. I felt less overwhelmed by my surroundings, and I felt an enormous difference in my attitude. I was able to cope with my past and move forward. Now, years later, the positive effects are still with me. I would never be as mentally and emotionally calm and readjusted to optimal living as I am now without neurofeedback.

61 ⌒ NUTRITION

Food is medicine. Food nourishes and heals the body. Eating well is central to the proper functioning of the human body, essential to our well-being. Do some research.

Talk with your practitioner or a nutritionist about how you can improve your diet. Don't worry about being perfect. Even small changes can bring great results. The best foods are those you can pick, grow, or catch, meaning vegetables, fruits, nuts, seeds, herbs, and lean meat. Keep it simple, and enjoy what is organic, not processed. Everyone's body is different, so listen to your body and make eating healthy a fun experience. It's not necessary for you to give up enjoying your food. Explore new foods and ways of eating. Your body will thank you for paying attention to what it needs and will be more able to heal.

62 ⌒ OIL PULLING

Oil pulling is a detoxification method used in Ayurvedic medicine that is accomplished by swishing oil in the mouth. The benefits are detoxification, healthier teeth and gums, and whiter teeth. In the morning on an empty stomach, before you drink anything, place a tablespoon of coconut, olive, or sesame oil in your mouth and gently swish it around for about 15-20 minutes, then spit it into the trash and rinse your mouth thoroughly. Be careful not to swallow the oil. After only a few weeks of oil pulling, I noticed my mouth felt cleaner, my teeth were whiter, and I felt a spring in my step. And every six months my dentist remarks how clean and healthy my mouth and teeth are. After doing this daily for a year, I now use it as a maintenance program once a week.

63 ⌒ ORGANIC

Going organic is better for your health. The more chemicals we allow into our food, the more harm and struggle we create for our bodies. Yes, it is more expensive, but we are worth it.

Do what you can and start slow. The most important items that need to be organic are foods that don't have protective layers, like berries and green leafy vegetables. Others like bananas, melons, or cucumbers can be peeled, so some of the harm from the chemicals can be avoided.

64 ⟲ OSTEOPATHY

Osteopathic therapy helps restore a person's health by focusing on the connection among the body's bones, muscles, organs, and nerves. A doctor of osteopathy (D.O.) treats the body as a collective whole. My primary doctor is a D.O. who has been instrumental in my healing. I get regular adjustments about every four to six weeks. The depth in which my symptoms are addressed and alleviated always amazes me. I left my last treatment feeling euphoric, with my body in alignment and my pain extinguished.

65 ⟲ PASSION

Prioritizing joy and passion in our life is an integral and direct path to health. In a day full of health challenges, we often neglect this most important ingredient. Living a passionate and creative life is rejuvenating. All systems of the body are positively affected when we make time for what fulfills us.

Every day when you wake up, think of one thing you are passionate about, whether it's drawing, having lunch with a friend, your happy and loyal pet, or a new hobby like gardening, jigsaw puzzles, juggling, baking, or the harmonica. Find something you can do that fills you with joy that you can't wait to do. I learned this from my great Uncle Roger, who always said that you've got to stay positive and have something in your life that you love doing. He's in his nineties now, and he paints, walks, works out at the gym, plays the saxophone in a band, and is probably more active on Facebook than I am.

66 ⁓ PETTING YOUR FURRY FRIENDS

The love and companionship of our furry friends can be both endearing and healing. When I pet my beautiful feline friend or my neighbor's dog, I am instantly cheered. Also, the vibrational purr of a cat has healing properties. But don't trust me; look it up and try for yourself. No, not you purring, but being with a cat that does. If you find that purring makes you feel better, then go for it. Perhaps you might do this at home. If you don't have a pet, consider rescuing one, or spending time at a shelter and petting the animals in need of love. You will both feel uplifted.

67 ⁓ PHYSICAL THERAPY

Physical therapists (PTs) help reestablish and maintain optimal movement and functional abilities of the human body and they often assist with treatment and rehabilitation from disease or injury. There are many areas that PTs focus on, such as orthopedic or cardiopulmonary, so it is important to find a PT best suited to your needs. I've had several over the years and it's a special relationship where both of you are invested in healing. With communication and determination, the results are often clear and lasting.

68 ⁓ PLAYING LIKE A CHILD

Somewhere along the way we can forget what it is like to be a child. To laugh, be silly, and play for no other reason than to play. Humans are creative beings who are meant to engage in joyful activities, use our imaginations, and feed our inner child, no matter our age. One of the best gifts I received when I was ill was a small container of bubbles from a close friend, one of the goofiest and loveliest people I know. When I opened this gift while lying in bed, I didn't know what to think. I had been a joyful, upbeat person, and goofy could have easily been my middle name, but I had lost that part of me. This inexpensive but endearing toy was exactly what I needed. I unscrewed the lid, took out the plastic stick dripping with that magic bubble liquid, and blew. Bubbles filled the air, and love filled my heart. Years later, this same friend bought me a Slinky for my birthday. It's on my bookshelf, next to my desk, ready to play when I need it.

69 ◌ POSITIVE THINKING

Thoughts are vibrations that affect us at a cellular level. When we are sick, it can be difficult to have an optimistic perspective. Learning to change our point of view can be a cornerstone in our healing. I have found the more positive I am, the better I feel, and I attract more positive energy and experiences. Being positive is truly one of the most magical and accessible tools in our health toolbox.

70 ◌ PRAYING

Prayer is a very personal experience. For some, it is not about religion, or even necessarily God, the universe, or a higher power. For some, it is. For me, prayer is feeling my connection to others and to some greater potential. Prayer for me is also feeling gratitude and projecting positive energy toward someone or something that needs my love, grace, or support.

During challenging times, prayer has always been uplifting and beneficial for me. I believe we are all connected to a greater source. And because we are all linked to something greater, we are also connected to each other. Prayer is always a source of feeling love and union and it is just a breath away. Illness and negative thoughts and emotions can temporarily give us the illusion of feeling separate. Prayer can bring us back to feeling love and connection.

71 ◯ PRIMAL SCREAMING

Primal screaming is a form of psychotherapy designed to release repressed pain and emotional distress from past traumas. Unlike traditional psychotherapy, this bypasses the reasoning areas of the brain and releases pain by getting in touch with the repressed feelings and then discharging them through deep breathing and screaming. At first, I felt uncomfortable engaging in this form of treatment. *Wait, I'm paying someone to help me scream?* Odd, yes, but after a few sessions with a primal scream expert (yes, they do exist), I had an intense and lasting breakthrough by releasing the pent-up anger and frustration I had from the traumas I had endured. I only had about six sessions, but I learned so much about myself, and I learned ways to release anger and frustrations that had been bottled up inside. Now, whenever I feel these emotions ready to burst, I grab my pillow and scream into it as loud and as uncensored as I can. It is a healthy release that always leaves me feeling so much lighter. Special note: If you are experiencing low energy, it may not be the best time to pursue this type of therapy, since it can be fatiguing.

72 ∽ PROBIOTICS

Probiotics live in the gut as live bacteria. They are fundamental to our vitality, most specifically for our immune and digestive systems. Illness, poor nutrition, environmental toxicity, and antibiotics cause us to lose a healthy balance within those systems. We can restore balance to healthy levels by taking high amounts and multiple strains of bacteria in the form of probiotics. You'll find probiotics at your local health food store or doctor's office, or online. Do your research and look for high-quality products that are well-packaged, since they are delicate substances and sensitive to heat, and be sure to find a reputable source. I take them every day and my gut has healed in many ways.

73 ∽ PURPOSE

Discovering your purpose, however great or small, can be a major turning point in your life. I've always wanted to be an athlete, student, world traveler, and writer, and for a while, I was all of those. However, when I fell ill, my identity was stripped away. I could no longer exercise, compete in sports, travel, study, or work. I felt lost, like I had no purpose.

One day, when I was distraught and lonely, believing I was worthless because I was sick all day, every day for years, unable to do anything, I rediscovered a new meaning to my life. Surrounded by all the love and grace of my friends and family, I realized that my sole purpose at that time was to love and be loved. I didn't need to do anything other than that. By reexamining my life and allowing my purpose to be fluid, I felt whole and worthy of being alive again. Feeling whole, connected, and purposeful is what led me to a more lasting and enduring healing. As I continue to heal, I am bringing other purposes in, like using writing to help and inspire others, always with the primary purpose of love.

74 READING

I know you're reading right now. And I thank you for that. Don't stop here. Keep expanding your reading to include a wide spectrum of topics to broaden your perspective and understanding of yourself and the world. Whether it is to escape, learn, or laugh, reading is a beautiful form of education and entertainment. Go to the library, borrow and trade with friends, join a book club or a poetry group, and pursue whatever piques your interest. Devouring the written word keeps your thoughts off your woes and sparks your imagination and creativity. Audiobooks or podcasts are a great option when you don't feel up to reading and were a significant help to me for a long time when I was too feeble to hold a book and focus my attention on the written words.

75 REIKI

Reiki, an ancient Japanese healing technique, is a spiritually guided life-force energy. A Reiki practitioner places their hands in certain positions either on or hovering over your body. The healing energy from the practitioner's hands restores vitality and promotes healing in the person receiving the treatment. This healing modality can be learned by anyone through classes and attunements received from a Reiki Master. It is gentle and yet powerful. After experiencing the full benefits of Reiki, I became a Reiki Master and feel humbled and honored by the beautiful exchange of energy and healing that comes from giving and receiving it. Imagine a massage for the mind, heart, and spirit—that is Reiki.

76 ○ RESTORATIVE YOGA

Restorative yoga is a gentle form of yoga, primarily for people with injuries or physical limitations. It is also generally soothing for anyone in need of restoration, which I am certain is everyone, unless you are the Buddha incarnate. Movements are done thoughtfully, and are sometimes supported by blankets, pillows, straps, and bolsters. Breathing techniques are emphasized to maximize the flow of oxygen and energy throughout the body. After restorative yoga, I always feel relaxed and renewed. Once you learn some of the basic poses, you can do them at home. Even just one a day is like a mini vacation.

77 ○ SAYING YES

When I was worn down from my myriad of health challenges, I stopped saying yes to living life fully. At one point during the height of my illness, I couldn't be left alone. I would shake and scream and cry from the pain and uncertainty of living with an undiagnosed illness. Everything was "no" and I was paralyzed by fear. It took time, but once I started on my trajectory of healing, one of the methods I employed was learning to acknowledge my fears and say yes to living again. Each time I did, I took a monumental leap forward. Soon, I no longer felt fearful when I was alone, and eventually I could walk to my mailbox, eat a new food, and experience new victories that reaffirmed that I could restore my health and live again. By saying no to the fear and yes to the beauty of life, I began regaining strength in all aspects of my being.

78 ᧢ SELF-LOVE

Besides gratitude, self-love is one of the most important practices you can adopt. It took me until my thirties, close to death, before I started loving myself. What a profound healing experience that was! Loving ourselves is the first step to acknowledging our humanness, accepting our past, readying ourselves for our future, and steadying ourselves for the moment. When we are anchored in self-love, we are giving our entire being—body, mind, and spirit—the recognition it deserves. We all came into this world as a child full of self-love. We need to reconnect with that and live from a place of esteem and devotion. That is the essence of health.

79 ᧢ SEX

Now I have your attention! Sex is a beneficial activity for obvious reasons. It can reduce stress, support the immune system, improve cardiovascular health, diminish pain, and help you sleep better. I don't advocate promiscuity, but getting physically close with your loved one can have several benefits. Whoever said getting healthy wasn't any fun? Even when you are not feeling well enough to make love, you can still engage in cuddling, closeness, and intimacy, which can be healing and connective.

80 ᧢ SHAMANIC HEALING

Speaking of sex (see #79), some people claim that prostitution is the oldest profession in the world. Actually, shamanism is. This ancient spiritual practice and form of healing is still a way of living in several cultures around the world. Shamanic healing works by identifying hidden causes for illness and energy imbalances. Once they are identified, a shaman conducts energetic movements, rituals, and healing sessions to remove, add, and restore energy. Some of my most profound mental, emotional, and spiritual breakthroughs came while seeing a shamanic healer. A session can include, for example, introspective probing of questions about your life, followed by drumming and what is called a shamanic journey that takes you into a guided meditative state. I've done this several times and experienced a depth of understanding and sense of tranquility that was rich and rewarding, something that I still draw from.

You may wonder where the heck you will find your friendly neighborhood shaman. Look on the Internet and ask your local spiritual center, health food store, or yoga center, or ask your friends. It may not be as easy as finding a YouTube video of cats doing adorable things, but they are out there. It's also important that you find someone you connect with and feel comfortable with, since it can often be an intimate and intense experience. Most of all, remember to be open.

81 ⟳ SIMPLIFYING

Different stressors in our lives amplify symptoms and create imbalances. Think of them like eggs in a basket. Too much stress and the eggs start to crack. By simplifying your life, you may be more at ease and have less stress. Limit your commitments and prioritize what you truly want from your life. What hobbies and activities do you enjoy? Which ones are no longer serving you? Make certain that any new activities you add are positive and helpful to your well-being. You will know because you'll look forward to that activity. If you dread something, let it go if you can. Less is actually more. When I started creating more space in my life with more time without something to do, I felt lighter and more balanced. In my case, I don't watch TV and I don't have cable. I don't miss it at all. This has been true for more than five years. Instead, I watch movies, read books, paint, meditate, spend time cooking, enjoying nature, and being with my friends. I also space out my commitments and things I say yes to. I always create space in my calendar for days off from doctor appointments, and for weekends where I don't open my computer or do any errands. It can all wait.

My days are more fluid, more joyful. I feel free and not shackled by having to do something every minute of every day. I now have more time, energy, and space to give more attention to the people and events that serve me best. The rest can fade away. Remember, we are mortal, not superheroes—even if you are wearing Underoos (Confused? See #49).

82 ⌒ SINGING

Singing is a wonderful activity that enables you to relax the muscles in your throat. It can open up the thyroid gland, which promotes healing. Sing in the shower, in the car with a friend, or while doing simple tasks at home. I do all three, and I don't judge how I sound. It's how I feel that matters (except to my neighbor's dog; he seems to care how I sound).

83 ⌒ SLEEPING AND RESTING

When I was young and healthy, functioning on less sleep became a bragging right. I used to push my limits and be proud of it. But then illness humbled me. A good night's sleep became imperative for my body to renew its energy and recover. Often we need quiet and solitude to restore our being without actually sleeping. Rest is what the doctor orders. Be kind to yourself and rest when your body asks you to. Value sleep and rest as much as you value oxygen. You can't live without it.

84 ⸰ SLEEPING HABITS

There is more to a restful night's sleep than climbing into bed and closing your eyes. I once did a sleep study to see if any disturbances in my sleep might be causing some of my symptoms. Fortunately, I did not have a sleep disorder, but the process was enlightening. A sleep specialist spent a long time explaining healthy sleep habits, so I changed my environment and routine. Over time, I noticed a definite change in my sleep: less interrupted; more soothing, and with fewer nightmares. Here are some of the many healthy sleep habits I learned:

- The bedroom is for sleep (and making love) only. Keep the television, computer, and other distractions out of it. I don't even read in bed anymore. Just sleep.

- Make your bedroom a clean, uncluttered, soothing place to be. It is a sanctuary for rest. The more inviting and calm the space is, the more restful your sleep.

- Sleep in darkness. It helps promote the natural rhythm of your sleep. The glow of light from alarm clocks and phones can disrupt total darkness.

- Turn off all electronic devices while sleeping, and optimally, stop using them an hour before you go to sleep.

- Sleep in quiet and peace and use earplugs if you have to. Sometimes soothing music can help lull you to sleep, but it is best to have silence.

- When possible, go to sleep around the same time each night, and wake around the same time each morning, which assists the circadian rhythm of the body.

- If you tend to have a racing mind at night, take a journal and write down all that is on your mind, scribbling until you can't write anymore. It helps clear your mind for sleep. Also, if you are thinking of all the things you have to do, make a list and put it in another room so you can rest soundly, knowing that you won't forget any of those items. They will be available the next day.

I follow every one of these sleep habits, and a few extra ones, like meditating before bed, and giving thanks for what happened throughout the day. These habits have made a lasting and positive difference in my health.

85 ⟲ STILLNESS

We live in a multitasking world, so it is rare that we sit in stillness. Even when our bodies are still, our mind can be in constant motion. For me, stillness is about sitting on the beach and watching the waves, noticing the moment, doing nothing—not even meditating. I take the attitude that I have nowhere to go, and nothing to do. Some people call it *The Art of Doing Nothing*, which is also the title of a fantastic book by Veronique Vienne. Whenever you can, practice doing absolutely nothing. Feel the freedom of taking a vacation from life. Even a few minutes can restore you in ways you never could have imagined. Embracing this concept is often difficult because modern life can keep us busy, but the busier we are, the more important this becomes. Stillness can also increase levels of happiness, lower your heart rate, increase brain function, and spark your imagination and creative side.

86 ⟳ STOP FIGHTING, START EMBRACING

For what seemed like the umpteenth time during my prolonged, crazy unknown chronic illness, I called 911 and was taken by ambulance from my home to the hospital with a heart rate of 195 beats per minute. As the sirens blared, the paramedic gave me nitrates, just in case I was having a heart attack. Unlike the many years I had spent fighting my illness, for the first time I shifted my perspective about my situation. Instantly, I felt calm, and I wasn't scared. I was alert and aware of the power of the moment. I was now paying attention. I closed my eyes and let go of the fight, which became the beginning of my true healing.

I learned to stop fighting my illness, accept the experience, and feel gratitude for the lessons, the love, all the assistance, and the adventure, as well as my body's ability to persevere and communicate with me. That moment in the ambulance was a pivotal point in my healing, where I stopped fighting my illness, my life, and my emotions, and started embracing and learning from them by living through them. No illusions here. It was not easy, but I wouldn't be alive if I hadn't made that shift.

87 ⌒ STRAIN AND COUNTERSTRAIN

Strain and counterstrain is a type of physical therapy designed to deeply realign the body. The physical therapist places your body in positions that exaggerate the imbalances in your body, enabling the body to adjust itself. Your muscles naturally realign, coming out of their habitual dysfunctional positions. Once the imbalances are addressed, the body can heal in those areas. For me, the results were often dramatic and almost instant. In one case I had a hiatal hernia, which is when the stomach has moved up into the chest area, past the diaphragm. It felt like someone shoved my stomach up under my ribcage, creating extreme tightness. I had trouble breathing, and I could not eat without the urge to vomit. In only one session, the strain and counterstrain expert identified the hiatal hernia, and using only his hands, was able to reposition and release my fascia and muscles to rectify the problem. The pain I had endured for almost two months was gone in one hour.

88 ⌒ STRETCHING

Stretching is important for your muscles because it keeps them loose and promotes proper functioning of your lymphatic and immune systems. It also creates more flexibility, which results in fewer injuries and improved performance during physical activities. Be mindful not to over stretch. Don't force yourself into positions. Just go to the edge of resistance where your body starts to tighten, and patiently breathe with acceptance until the muscles release. I suggest you attend a stretching or gentle yoga class to learn about light stretches you can do at home. Think cats. They are always stretching, and look how limber they are. But note: just because you start stretching and doing gentle yoga, doesn't mean you will be able to jump straight up on to the top of a fence and bend the way cats do, or chase your tail. Sad, but true.

Since I started stretching every day, my body feels stronger, and I am able to do certain activities I couldn't do before. For example, when I bent forward, I used to be able to barely touch the tops of my feet. Now I can place my hands flat on the floor, and my hamstrings are much more relaxed. I may not be doing the limbo anytime soon, but I can certainly feel the lengthening of my muscles and the freedom to move easier through my daily activities.

89 ⟳ Student for Life

The world is our classroom and we are constantly learning. Often, our most difficult life experiences teach us the most. It is advantageous to remember this at our most trying times, since just by bringing our awareness to that understanding, we can alter those experiences. Know also that pain is a teacher, and it is temporary. Keep your mind and eyes open.

Once I began doing this, I saw life in a different way. Once, another car cut me off on the freeway, causing my car to crash at fifty-five miles per hour. I ended up with a skull fracture and was in a neck brace and in physical therapy for almost a year. It was traumatic, but I learned so much from what happened. I realized that there are not good and bad experiences, just lessons. This took me a while to master, and I am still challenged by it from time to time, but it works. Change your perspective, and you can change your circumstances.

90 ⌒ SUPPLEMENTS

It is difficult for us to get all of the nutrition we need from the food we eat. Our nutritional needs are individualized. Nutritional supplements can provide essential vitamins and minerals that you may be lacking. Since there are many types and brands, discuss supplementation with a nutritionist or a doctor who has studied nutrition. Saying that, less is often more. Be selective about what you choose and from what company, since not all supplements are created equal. I like to vary what I take and keep current on understanding what my body needs as it changes. Lab tests can help you identify what you need most. I also advocate trying one new supplement at a time and starting with a low dose, so you can see how you react. If you feel like you're doing well, you can add more. Some basics to consider are digestive enzymes and probiotics for your gut health, vitamin D for the immune system, and vitamin B12 to support the nervous system.

91 ⌒ SUPPORT GROUPS

Talking to people who are going through or have gone through what you have can be an invaluable experience. Being undiagnosed for so long, it was difficult for me to find an appropriate support group, but I learned to talk with people who had been through similar situations, and that helped. There are many online forums where you can find support. One I used is *Daily Strength*. Whatever support you find, be mindful not to use the group in a way that makes your illness your identity. Remember, you may have an illness, but it doesn't define who you are.

92 ⊙ TEAMWORK

Being ill can be lonely. Having a team to support you, guide you, love you, and dispense advice to you is critical to healing. Surround yourself with people who encourage and love you. Ask them to be a part of your healing team. The same goes with doctors, healers, and any type of medical practitioner. Find ones who are dedicated to helping you, those who truly listen and see you and what you are going through. At certain points throughout my health challenges, I encountered physicians and practitioners who were dismissive, curt, didn't listen, and sometimes condescending. In the beginning, I was influenced by them and somehow thought my illness was my fault. Then I realized it wasn't anything I had done. I needed to stand up for myself and find the people who would support me in positive ways. If a member of your team is discouraging or destructive, or in any way prohibits healing, find a gentle way to let that relationship go, and find another team member who is positive and supportive. Having a loyal team in place keeps you fully supported and able to focus on what you need to do: heal.

93 ⊙ TRUSTING YOUR INSTINCTS

Following your intuition is another way of saying, "trust your instincts." It took me a long time to fully comprehend that I can trust that intuitive knowing I have, when faced with a difficult circumstance, decision, or emotion. When I sense my gut reacting to something, I listen and practice heeding it. The more you do this, the more in tune you can be with your best and highest needs. Our gut knows what we need, and when we listen to it, we benefit and can heal.

94 ○ Unplugging

Taking time away from our electronic devices is an important part of healing. We have come to rely on our computers, phones, televisions, and other gadgets. Yet, it is unnatural to spend excessive time with technology. The artificial electromagnetic fields (EMF) generated from all of these devices can cause health problems. Unplug for an hour or two, especially at night before bed. I like to take Sundays off completely. I always feel better. I know it's not easy, but by unplugging you are gaining back a part of your natural human state and giving your body and mind a chance to relax and, well, reboot. On a positive note, when I do use media, I choose podcasts, meditations, and films that enrich my life.

95 ○ Visualization

Visualization is a powerful method of connecting with yourself at a deeper level and releasing inner feelings that may be blocking your healing process. Find a comfortable chair, cushion, or bed, then close your eyes and visualize yourself in positive, relaxing ways. Imagine your body as a strong entity that is vibrant and healthy. These thoughts can create actual physiological changes in the body.

There are ways to use visualization to help you heal. For instance, you can even travel to exotic, peaceful locations in your mind and gain all the benefits without leaving the comfort of your own space. Your brain will interpret the experience like you've actually traveled there. I like to go to Tahiti. I just close my eyes, and within a few minutes I'm on a sandy beach, sipping a fruity drink, feeling the gentle ocean breeze against my skin while watching the glow of the sunset. You won't collect any frequent flyer miles or be able to bring back a T-shirt with a pineapple on it, but hey, we can't have everything.

96 ⌒ VOLUNTEERING

A wonderful way to heal is to give back to others who are less fortunate. There is always someone who needs help and assistance. When I was healthy, I used to do a lot of volunteer work. When I was ill, I felt horrible that I was unable to give back. I couldn't do much, but I found something that I could do. I started going to a private animal shelter where I sat on the ground in a cage and petted all the cats that were lonely and wanted affection. What a magnificent feeling to help those beautiful felines. When you give back, even in the smallest ways, your problems are put in perspective and you become grateful for all that you do have. Small acts with great love are the most important. A smile, a hug, a compliment, some compassion, anything that can be given and shared is a beautiful exchange of positive energy that invigorates you and those you are helping.

97 ⌒ WALKING

Walking is one of the best exercises anyone can do. Not only is it the most natural, but it opens up the energy of your body and helps the lymphatic system function better, which is vital to cleaning toxins out of your body and supporting the immune system. Even just five minutes at a time helps. Walk in natural settings like the beach, a trail, or a park, which also brings you closer to nature and creates a better flow of oxygen while engaging your other senses. If you have limited mobility like I do sometimes, try emulating walking with your arms while seated. On days when I just don't have the energy, I do a visualization that I'm walking in my favorite spot down at the beach or near a lake or lagoon. Even just a simple walk across the street and back will help. The point is to move. If you sit a lot, then at the top of the hour get up and walk around the house; then at the next top of the hour, do it again. It's just enough to keep the blood flowing, which is imperative for healing.

98 ○ WATER

Our bodies are composed of 60% water. Drinking adequate water each day is vital to our well-being, so drink it up. If you can, replace sodas and coffee (which dehydrate you) with water. If you don't like drinking water, try putting lemon, lime, or orange slices in it, or mint, cucumber, or strawberries. I have sparkling water with a lime in it as a treat, always in a fancy glass to make myself feel like I'm drinking a fun, fancy beverage. In the end, hydration is the cornerstone to maintaining good health.

99 ○ WELLNESS WORDS

Words are powerful. Words are vibration. Words create our reality. Pay attention to the words you use and what you think. It is important to focus on positive, happy words, feelings, and emotions whenever possible. Each word matters, so choose happiness. Avoid words and phrases like *I should, I have to, I can't, I need to work on, I used to, I hate,* or *this is killing me.* Replace them with more positive ones such as *I would like to focus on, I feel like doing this, I believe in myself, I know I can, I embrace,* and *this is an adventure, challenge,* or *life lesson that I will learn from.* With practice, you can create new, positive word habits.

100 ⌒ Whatever Works

I'm not kidding. I firmly believe in whatever works. If someone told me to stand on my head, drink celery juice, and watch videos of sea otters for twenty minutes, every day for three months, and I tried it and it worked, then it was worth looking silly and fielding tons of questions like, "Have you completely lost your mind?" My point is, whatever works, for whatever reason it works, cannot always be understood. Sometimes we have to take a leap of faith and try, and if it helps, awesome! It was worth it. If it doesn't, at least you tried, and you probably learned a few things you can pass along to those in your same boat. Remember, it's not always important to know the why and how, as long as you achieve the right results. Let me tell you, I walk my talk. *A Few Minor Adjustments* demonstrates just how far and absurd I was willing to go to heal. It was a crazy experience, and I learned so much. What worked? You'll have to read the book to find out.

Don't let your story
have power over you.
You can change.
Let go of your story.
Enter the unwritten.

ACKNOWLEDGMENTS

Thank you to my team for your incredible support and belief in me and this project. I am grateful for your expertise and enthusiasm. To my writing group: Thanks for all your sage critiques and for always making me laugh along the way. To Anna-Marie Abell: Thanks for being my buddy in all this writing craziness. You've made it a much more enjoyable ride. To Matthew Pallamary: I treasure your continued counsel and feedback for this and all my writing endeavors. To Asa Wild: Both this book, and my life, would not be as beautiful without you. Thank you for your creativity and kindness.

To all the doctors and other healers who have taught me, and countless others, the true nature of healing. You have my profound appreciation and gratitude. Special thanks to Dr. Melinda Nevins, Willow MacPherson, and Shelley McQuerter for your valuable insight on this project. You have enhanced this book and continue to enrich my life.

Thank you to my friends and family for your unwavering love and devotion throughout my life. Because of you, my heart is full and healed at the deepest level.

Finally, to my readers and all those in need of healing, thank you for coming with me on this journey. May you experience healing and happiness in every moment and may you savor the beauty of being alive.

ABOUT THE AUTHOR

Raised in Venice, California, Cherie longed to travel and experience the way other people lived. After serving as a Peace Corps volunteer in Zambia on a water sanitation and health education project, Cherie returned to the United States with an African souvenir she didn't expect: a mysterious illness. She fell severely ill and almost died, leaving her with several symptoms that went undiagnosed for many years. This inspired Cherie to write her memoir, *A Few Minor Adjustments: A Memoir of Healing*, taking the reader on a powerful but entertaining journey through her adventures and search for life-saving answers.

Her memoir has won several awards and received an outpouring of heartfelt responses, motivating Cherie to write a companion book, *The Healing 100: A Practical Guide to Transforming Your Body, Mind, and Spirit*.

Cherie has earned a Masters in Medical and Cultural Anthropology and has been celebrated for her holistic approach to healing and her willingness to examine her life lessons in her writing.

Stay connected at: CherieKephart.com

ALSO BY

CHERIE KEPHART

A Few Minor Adjustments: A Memoir of Healing

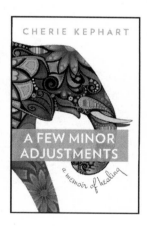

Take
a
look
inside!

the first two chapters of...

A FEW MINOR ADJUSTMENTS
a memoir of healing

CHERIE KEPHART

BAZI
PUBLISHING

chapter one

ENTERING
THE UNKNOWN

APRIL 2004, PART I – SAN DIEGO

Hard water hit my breasts. The musty odor of old pipes filled my nostrils. I coughed and turned in circles in my shower, observing the cracked tiles beneath my feet, stepping carefully around them because I had been cut before. I avoided the large patches of mold covering the rusty handles and walls. No matter how much I scrubbed, this cottage was run-down and full of spores.

Damn landlord never fixes a thing.

I lathered my skin with soap, breathing in the scent of citrus as I scoured the crevices that had collected sand from playing beach volleyball earlier that evening. The image of Alex entered my mind; his short brown hair, crystal-blue eyes, full ruby lips, and olive skin. I envisioned his tall, lean, and muscular body pressing up against me as we made love. I had only known him for a few months, but we were enamored with one another. We met while I was working as a technical writer at a software company. We became friends, sharing our adoration for animals, love for exercise, thirst for intellectual conversation, and desire to spend quiet time in nature. My thirty-third birthday was in a few weeks and I wondered what we would do to celebrate.

I turned to rinse the soap from my back and felt a sharp biting pain in my neck. I dropped to the hard tile floor. Water pounded over my head. I tried to stand, to move my neck, but the pain intensified like a saw ripping my flesh and muscles apart. I screamed.

I crawled out of the shower and across the floor.

Focus. Get to the phone. Call for help.

I inched across the living room floor, one arm limp by my side, the other forcing me along like an oar wading through sand. I reached the phone and dialed.

Pick up. Please.

"Hello?"

"Alex?" My voice felt shallow. My wet hand gripped the receiver.

"Cherie. You all right?"

"No." I strained to speak. "Intense pain. I collapsed." I forced words into the air between breaths. "My neck feels— broken. I don't know how, but I can't feel my left arm. I'm scared, Alex."

"Hang on, CK, I'll come right over."

I dropped the phone. I had suffered chronic throbbing neck pain for years from a car accident when I was twenty-one, but this felt as if a lion had ripped apart my neck with its teeth. I inched from the kitchen back to the bathroom. Heard the water still running from the shower. I pushed along the rough hardwood floor. Long, sopping hair covered my face.

My concentration weakened. Heat radiated from my neck into my limbs. My legs burned.

Just get to the bathroom.

My arms and legs quivered. I pushed myself up using both sides of the door jamb. I entered the cramped, steamy shower. Turned the handle enough to halt most of the flowing water. The shower head continued to drip, but I didn't care.

I groaned, forcing myself down the corridor to my bedroom. Holding my neck with my right hand, I climbed wet and naked onto the mattress. My neck stiffened as if my muscles were filled with cement. From the corner of my eye I saw my digital alarm clock on the nightstand, but the numbers looked hazy: 8, 4, 5. 8:45 p.m. The drive from Alex's studio apartment would be at least thirty minutes. Would I make it that long?

Goose bumps prickled across my arms and legs. I wrapped myself in a golden throw that hung over the edge of the bed. The dampness of my skin made me tremble. I swayed back and forth in tiny movements and started to cry.

A tidal wave of tension rushed through me. I grimaced and turned toward the clock. 8:52. *Please hurry, Alex* echoed in my head like a mantra.

I thought back to my visit to the hospital two weeks earlier. The ER smelled like bleach and fear. Fluorescent lights shone brightly overhead. I sat on a gurney in a busy hallway and watched the flurry of activity. My knee ached and my heart pounded like an elephant stampeding after too much Red Bull and cocaine. Something was wrong with me and I trusted that the medical system would agree and offer me an efficient way to heal.

A red-haired doctor with bushy eyebrows rushed up to me. "What did you find?" I asked him.

He paused, shaking his head. "Your EKG's a bit, well, unusual," said Dr. Unsure, as I had come to think of him.

Just say it, I can take it.

"It's your heart. Your EKG readings are reversed." He fiddled with his stethoscope.

"What's that mean?"

"I'm not sure," said Dr. Unsure. "Very unusual." He scratched his head, thought for a moment. "I've never seen this before, but I don't believe there's anything to worry about right now."

So, the time to worry would be when?

"I need you to do a follow-up with your primary doctor, a cardiologist, and a neurologist. You seem stable enough for now."

Stable enough?

I drove home with fifty less dollars in my checking account and a thousand more worries.

Sharp stinging sensations crept up my neck to the base of my head, bringing me back to the moment. Still in my cottage. 9:01. My hands shook as I propped myself up. The wet blanket fell to the floor. I stumbled toward my closet, panting as I shoved clothes aside with my right arm, searching for a loose T-shirt and sweatpants. I situated the shirt around my neck and torso; the cotton fabric stuck to my damp breasts. I struggled, pulling down the shirt, still crying, still shaking.

I bent over to lift my sweatpants, fumbled with my left leg, then dropped my right leg gingerly into the hole, and finally pulled the pants up around my waist.

Shoes. Easy shoes. I slid my feet into my sandy flip flops.

What else? ID. Insurance card. Purse.

I turned toward the hallway, and a bolt of pain sledgehammered my neck. I grabbed my head and fell to the floor.

Red numbers glowed out of the corner of my eye. 9:15. The clock mocked me. I dragged myself toward the living room. My purse dangled on the edge of a chair. I stretched out toward the bag, grabbed it, and crumpled onto the carpet. I tried to inhale but could only produce curt, shallow breaths.

Please, someone help me!

I heard a car door slam. Harnessing strength, I pushed myself up from the floor and limped to the door.

Alex's voice sounded muffled through the thick wooden door. "Cherie. Open up."

I wanted to scream out to him, but my voice was a breathless rasp. I cried as I unlocked and pulled the door open.

Alex towered over me. His luminous blue eyes sparkled between his thick eyelashes, and a hazy white cloud highlighted his body. He looked like a savior. He stretched out his arms and gently wrapped them around me. I shook and sobbed. "What happened?" he asked.

"I don't know."

"I've got you, CK. Hang on." He lifted me into his arms and carried me to the car.

In the waiting room, Alex held me close and consoled me. The masculine aroma of perspiration and shampoo filled my nostrils as I nestled in his arms. I could feel the compassion in his touch. A serious man, Alex was a software engineer who had worked his way up to vice-president of a Fortune

500 company. A self-proclaimed "unforgiving bastard," but I had come to know his softer side. He often spent weekends volunteering at animal shelters, rescuing stray cats and finding them homes.

The emergency room bustled with activity. Nurses scurried from one side of the waiting area to the other. I surveyed the people around me and noticed a faint scent of blood. A disheveled, burly man with a stab wound sat alone staring at the floor, holding a blood-soaked wash cloth on the side of his stomach. Was it a bar fight, gang related, or some form of fatal attraction?

A quiet middle-aged Hispanic couple sat across from me. I couldn't discern the reason for their visit to the ER, or which one of them was sick. They watched me periodically, perhaps wondering what pathogen I had, and what, if anything, I infected their air with.

Was I contagious?

Alex kept his eyes on me, occasionally running his hand along my back or across my leg. His presence kept me sane.

We sat for hours in our awkward plastic waiting-room chairs. I focused on wanting to live, yet the pangs radiating from my neck and head raged as if a savage battle were being fought over my every muscle, sinew, and bone.

"Why's it taking so long? I can't stand this anymore."

"I know. This is awful. I'll ask the nurse again. You've got to hang on, CK."

Although Alex sat next to me, I somehow felt alone. He knew about the two other times I'd endured pain so overpowering that, unlike this day when I fought to live, I asked to die.

My heart rate accelerated as I recalled those times of despair and what I had survived. Did those two episodes give me the strength to overcome this new trial, or had they depleted my reservoir of endurance? Had they contributed to my current unknown condition?

I didn't know.

chapter two

PIONEERING
FOR PEACE

I was twenty-three years old the first time I wished for death. I was serving as a Peace Corps volunteer in Zambia. Twelve of us became the first group of volunteers. We would learn to speak the Bantu language, Bemba. We called ourselves the *Kalapashi*, meaning "the pioneers."

Before traveling to Africa, I absorbed the Peace Corps medical spokesperson's lecture on a multitude of precautions, preventive measures, consequences, and statistics. She described several diseases, emergencies, injuries, and accidents we were bound to encounter throughout our two-year service.

Each year millions of people around the world were infected with malaria. Between one and three million people died from this parasitic infection. Ninety percent of these deaths occurred in Africa. Besides the high risk of contracting malaria, HIV was prevalent. Statistics showed that approximately eighty-five percent of Peace Corps volunteers had sexual relations while in their host country. Heterosexual transmission of HIV in the United States represented eight percent. In Africa, it was eighty percent. There were thirteen million cases of HIV in the world. Eight million of those were in Africa. Fifty percent of hospital patients there had HIV. Hospitals and medical clinics commonly reused needles for immunizations and blood drawing because supplies were low. Instead of sterilizing, they washed the needles in hot water.

Aside from warning us about venomous snakes, crocodiles, and spiders, they warned us about dysentery, giardia, hepatitis, and a wide variety of water-borne diseases like schistosomiasis. Equipped with all of this staggering information, I assured myself that for the duration of my service I would always boil and treat my drinking water (even before brushing my teeth), consistently take my prophylactic medications, sleep in a chemically treated mosquito net, stay current on my immunizations, abstain from sex, keep out of hospitals and medical clinics, and avoid swimming in any body of water.

Being young, unhampered, and idealistic, I decided I would remain healthy by adhering to the rules and guidelines and remain conscious of everything I did. My young mind propelled me forward without fear. I joined the Peace Corps because I aspired to make my life mean something. I needed to believe I was imperishable. I kept thinking of a quote from Margaret Mead: "Never doubt that a group of thoughtful, committed citizens can change the world. Indeed, it's the only thing that ever has."

I wanted to be a part of that change. Never did I imagine that most of the change would be within me.

My first three months, from January to April, were with my eleven fellow volunteers in the south of Zambia, participating in language, technical, and cultural training. Each of us lived with a host family. Since Zambia had been a British colony, many of the locals in the larger cities spoke English. At the end of our three-month training we would be relocated to remote villages where almost only Bemba would be spoken.

During our training, we lived in Kabwe, an old zinc and lead mining town. Home to 200,000 residents, it offered few amenities. The middle of town had a large marketplace where hundreds of local vendors sold their agricultural and homemade goods. It smelled like charcoal and dust, surrounded by a steady stream of flies constantly circling and landing on the makeshift tables, food, and people. The training site, where we studied and gathered for Peace Corps events, was on the outskirts.

We were trained to orchestrate water and sanitation/ health education projects; to build wells and latrines; and to educate the locals about good health practices to prevent disease. When I arrived, people bathed in, drank out of, urinated, and defecated near and in the same slow moving river that ran through the village. The degree of illness and death from contaminated water sources was alarming. Combined with deaths from malaria, HIV, and other causes, the average life expectancy of Zambians was around thirty-two years.

Despite my cautious intentions, illness managed to find me in interesting ways. In addition to changes in diet, such as fried caterpillars that tasted similar to burnt French fries, and newly found bowel functions that all of the volunteers enjoyed, I noticed three red sores, one on the inside of my right arm and two on my behind. At first they looked like pimples, so I ignored them, but after a few weeks, they grew bigger, darker red, and became so piercing it was difficult to sit.

The Peace Corps medical staff, a doctor and nurse who were both in Zambia for the first time, brought me into a small unused dorm room on the Peace Corps training campus to investigate the sores. The room smelled musty, had cold concrete floors and one window that was painted shut.

"Cherie, lie down on that cot and we'll take a look at you," Dr. Enthusiasm said, pointing to a child-sized mattress in the corner. He was a brown-haired Jerry Garcia look-a-like from Alabama. I wondered if he had ever been to a Grateful Dead concert. The nurse, a petite and naturally beautiful dark-haired woman from Alaska, smiled at me.

I positioned myself on the bed, lying backside up, and lowered my pants and underwear so they could see the two bright red sores on my butt. The two medical professionals rubbed, poked, and picked at the sores, chatting back and forth while I kept from fidgeting.

"We aren't certain, but we think you've contracted a Putzi fly or Tumbu fly infection. This is exciting." The doctor's voice cracked. "I've never seen it before, but I just read about it. It's native to Africa. The flies lay eggs in damp clothes hanging outside to dry. Once the clothes come into contact with human skin, the eggs hatch. The larvae burrow into the skin and, if left untreated, morph into adult maggots."

"Whoa. Did you say maggots?"

"Yes, maggots."

The muscles in my stomach tightened. "I have maggots in my butt?"

"It's been a few weeks since you first noticed them, correct?"

"Yes. But, oh gosh, how do we get them out?"

"We'll have to cut them out. It may be a little painful. You'll have to remain quite still, all right?"

I reached my arms up to grasp the thin metal frame of the bed. I shut my eyes. "Okay."

While the doctor rubbed the areas with a cold, wet antiseptic wipe, I braced myself. They used an X-Acto blade and a pair of tweezers, medical instruments resembling those included with the board game Operation.

The sharp blade cut into my flesh. Lying face down, I couldn't see what they were doing with these elementary tools, but it sounded like an archaeological investigation being conducted on my butt cheeks.

"That's interesting. Wait, I have it. Nope, I lost it. Wait, I have it. No, it burrowed back in again. We've got to cut a little more. Okay, now dig." Their less than comforting dialogue, coupled with their probing and cutting, continued for almost forty-five minutes, during which I thought so many things. What was I doing here? Maybe I made a mistake? Who was I kidding? Get these things out of me! Was I strong enough for this? Was I prepared? How does one prepare for getting maggots in her butt? I knew that the Peace Corps experience was not for the weak hearted, but I didn't know it was going to be this tough. I was not in a hospital or a medical clinic (which I wanted to avoid, so how could I complain?), but in a random, non-sterile room with no pain medication in sight. Just me, two perplexed medical staff with tools from their portable first-aid kit, and three determined worms.

"We've got it!" they exclaimed when they finally extracted the first maggot from my aching ass. "Do you want to see it?"

I was not in the mood for show and tell. But they showed me a cream-colored worm about a half an inch long wriggling on the end of the tweezers before I had a chance to respond. It looked about as happy as I did.

"Do you need to take a break or should we continue?"

My glute muscles ached as if they had been stung by a swarm of wasps. "No break, let's get the other two out of me." I closed my eyes and waited for the cold, sharp blade to once again cut into the fatty flesh on my behind.

The second one didn't take as long, perhaps ten minutes total.

"Not too much blood. That wasn't bad," they said to me with mild excitement.

My butt cheeks didn't agree, but with only one worm left in my body, I felt relieved. After they cleaned the areas and placed bandages on the two holes, I pulled up my underwear and pants and turned onto my side so they could address the last worm in my arm. I felt nauseated and fidgeted.

The nurse held my arm as the doctor picked at my flesh with the small, shiny blade. "Okay, hold still."

"I'm trying."

"Sorry, Cherie, not you, the worm."

"Oh."

"I have it," Dr. Enthusiasm said. "Oh no. That's not good."

I looked at my bicep where the freeloading worm vacationed, but the nurse and doctor hovered over me, and I couldn't see what they were doing. "What happened?"

"Ah. I grabbed a hold of it, but I think it broke in half. See?" The lifeless half worm sprinkled in blood drooped on the tweezers.

"Where's the other half?"

The nurse swallowed and with a sheepish expression said, "I think it went back in your arm."

Having half of a worm inside me felt worse than having the whole thing. What if it couldn't be retrieved? What would happen then?

I felt beads of sweat form on my back. I wanted Dorothy's ruby slippers to click me back to the time before maggots invaded my flesh. After more excavating and tweezing, the other half of the worm eventually came out of my arm.

The next day, the nurse explained that she had researched further into Putzi fly infections.

"It turns out they are easily prevented and treated," the nurse said with a proud voice. "To prevent them, you must iron all of your clothes. The heat kills the eggs and stops them from making their way into your skin. To remove a worm, spread Vaseline on the infected area. It cuts off the air supply to the maggot. In order not to suffocate, it comes out on its own."

"Wait. If we had simply spread a dollop of Vaseline on my skin, the maggots would have come out on their own?"

"It seems so. Well, at least now we know." The nurse sported a half grin.

Just call me Guinea, last name Pig.

My encounter with these little scrounging creatures prevented others from suffering the same fate. John, one of my fellow volunteers, was a twenty-three-year-old New Yorker who was deaf since a young age, had wavy brown hair, clear-rimmed glasses and hearing aids, and always wore long pants, long-sleeved shirts, and sweatshirts with hoods. He often removed his hearing aids, covered his head with his hood, and tuned out the world.

John's words came soft, lower than a whisper. "Cherie, what did the nurse say?"

I mouthed, "Iron all clothes."

He looked confused. "Really?"

"Yup. Another item to add to the must-do list." I giggled.

He smiled and gave me a warm, comforting hug.

It was a lesson I only needed to learn once, but without electricity, this was not an easy task. After hand-washing and line-drying my clothes, I used a coal iron over each article, including socks, bras, underwear, and even shoelaces. Laundry day became an all-day event, but it was worth the effort. My clothes looked nicely pressed, and more importantly, I was maggot-free.

By April, I had completed my three-month training and felt ready to apply what I had learned. Eager to help improve the water and waste management of the villagers I had yet to meet, my impassioned enthusiasm clouded the details of what lay ahead. I didn't envision living in an isolated village, not knowing anyone, digging wells and latrines in the hot African sun surrounded by disease and death. I envisioned hope, friendship, peace, and health.

STAY INVOLVED

CONNECT WITH CHERIE ON HER WEBSITE

CherieKephart.com

WRITE A REVIEW

for *The Healing 100*
CherieKephart.com/review

CONNECT WITH CHERIE ON SOCIAL MEDIA

@Cherie.Kephart.Author

Cherie Kephart

@CherieKephart

@CherieKephartWriter